How to Draw Capital

Letters

Uppercase

ÍNDICE

Lettering, caligrafía and tipografía

Letter Anatomy

Drawing Letters

introduction

In 1535, the artist Albrecht Dürer invented a way to describe the structure of letters for design and reproduction.

Imagine that you. you're on the phone with a person who has never seen the alphabet. This person understands basic concepts, like "square" circle "and" line ", but has no idea how to make an" A ", or" "B" or any other letter. Do you think it possible to explain over the phone, using just those simple terms, how to draw all the letters?

Sounds easy ?, try with "B." A straight line with two semi-circles ?, this description is far from sufficient; a line from where to where ?, where do the semicircles go ?, and what is a semicircle? is not easy.

And if instead of a general form of the "B" ,. Should you explain to this person how to make a perfect "B" in Times? O Palatino? Or in Trajan letters or another typeface? It seems impossible, luckily the occasion of having to give verbal instructions for precise letters is very rare.

I accept that this need comes, millions of times per second. When a computer loads digital fonts, these are not just "pictures" of the letters, they are very complex verbal instructions on how to draw precise letters. A computer has no idea what is a "B", to display a "B", read and follow the instructions in the digital font.

Dürer did not have a computer, but he had the idea to describe how the letters of the Roman alphabet are drawn, to understand and work on their structure, using only simple terms such as square, circle and line.

Dürer's 23-letter alphabet (J, U, and W are not used in Latin) was quite elegant. Many other artists published elegant alphabets before him, what made the book special was Dürer's eccentric idea that the instructions for the construction of the letters should be fully described in geometric form.

The book was illustrated with samples of each letter, but the point is that you could draw those letters yourself, precisely and perfectly without seeing the illustrations. Dürer had invented science in typography. and if the achievements of this artist were not so extensive, he would be remembered only for that book.

The proportions of the letters, when designed together, require a basic proportional regime that is common to all, which are the height lines or segments. In the first alphabets, less developed, the letters were more "loose in space", since only in some formal writings did he worry about a detailed alignment and the concordance of all sizes, and the cases in which they were considered, were made evident, since they had very marked guide lines above and below that were part of the visible structure, the alphabet then was not designed to solve this by itself, except for some increasingly frequent cases in which the order of the page was favored , dividing the space in a more efficient way.

The more advanced cases, which point towards the minuscules, define the proportions of three zones; central, ascending and descending, the height of each zone defines many aspects of the design, since they delimit the basic shapes of the total image defining the primary proportions of all the letters together and balance, some more recent designs are based on specific mathematical proportions of the construction of the design to define the heights and ensure an optimal ratio that favors reading, much more precise than manual writing. The mechanical reproduction of a modern alphabet favors the use of more detailed proportions, and the fulfillment of these.

Lettering, Calligraphy and Typography

Calligraphy
The art of writing letters

The Calligraphy is the basis of everything. Both the lettering and the typography are based on this, since over the years it has evolved. In fact, there are as many styles of calligraphy as there are people, since their main function is solely to write.

In calligraphy is the technique. It is a hand art, based on a grid and an alphabet, whose set of characters must have harmony, rhythm and fluidity. Calligraphy is based on alphabets from different times, the founding alphabet is the basis of modern calligraphy, and the book *The Foundational Hand* to it is the starting point for anyone who wants to enter the world of calligraphy.

Once you master this basic alphabet and its technique, you can add touches of your personality to the letters until you find your own alphabet, to make it totally unique.

The Foundational Hand

Práctica d ela caligrafía

The calligraphy is traditionally carried out with a calligraphic pen and any ink (in black ink or watercolors). Everything is completely different, no matter how much you try to imitate, it is easy to see when it is calligraphy and when it is not.

You will notice that each letter is unique. It is the good to write by hand, that never, ever, will come out of letters completely equal. That's what gives it its distinctive touch and personality.

Another characteristic is the contrast of the letters that appears naturally due to a broad pen.

The Foundational Hand, is a very good initial calligraphy guide to start. Before starting in the lettering, it is of fundamental importance a quick introduction to the world of calligraphy. The book is translated into several languages and available on Amazon:

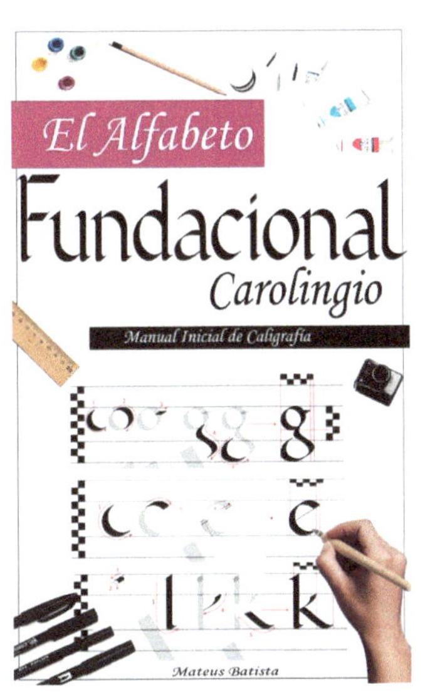

Typography

The art of stamping letters

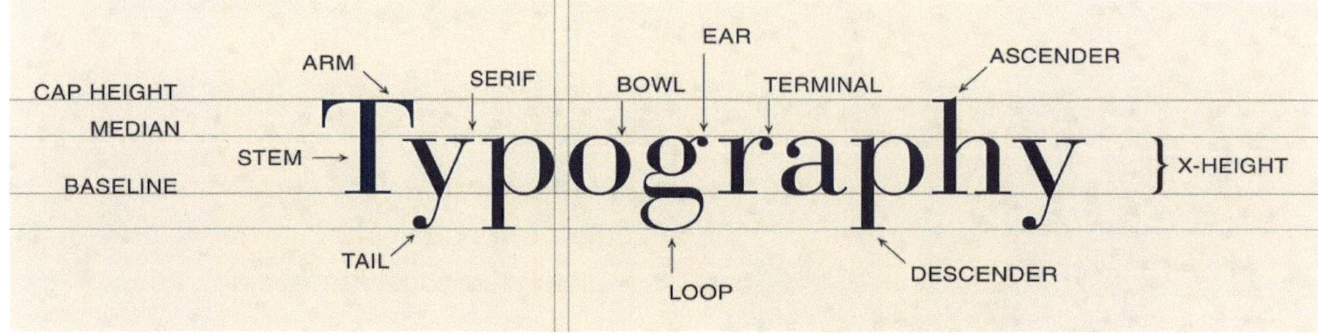

The typography is a character set with a design designed and studied specifically to be programmed and used in another computer. There is no possibility of making a typography by hand.

So, whatever you install in your computer, it is a typography. Today, given the multitude of typefaces that exist, there are many that try to imitate the calligraphy and lettering. But never the in the same way. The typography will always have this imperfectional that can be achieved with other techniques.

If you want a calligraphy or true lettering, choose it, because it has the magic and the imperfection that does not find in a typography that tries to imitate them. When you are in front of a lettering or original calligraphy or typography, look at the letters that are repeated. If they are completely the same, you are in front of a typography.

I urge you to become emphatic from my mism to picking up a view of all the letters that you find in your day to see if you are able to differentiate them.

Lettering

The art of drawing letters

When the calligraphy goes further, and instead of writing, it intends to give, decorate, create shapes with the letter, pass the calligraphy to lettering. The lettering is the art of drawing letters.

In the moment in which you "deform", the biggest thing, you change the shape of a letter so that it makes you more beautiful in relation to the rest (for example, interlaced we bring descendants, many times the ascending of the letter L so that you don't shock other letters, etc.).

The lettering field is much more subjective and personal than the calligraphy, so here, really, every one should give his style to his letters. Just like with the calligraphy, in the lettering also out of the equal letters. Of course, if you try to vary the shape of the letters, in case they are repeated very often, so that you can clearly see that it is close by.

The lettering can be done with any writing material. From brushes with watercolors, labelers, pencils, boligraphers, and even digitalizing them with Adobe Illustrator.

With Ruler

and Compass

In this work we will approach a different lettring from the usual one, we will delve into lines and mathematical rules for drawing letters for posters or signs.

The designer should study the proportions of the components of the signs, in particular the relationship between width and height, the widths of capital letters, the relationship between heights of uppercase, lowercase, the location of the waist of the signs.

It is convenient to analyze the structural relationships between uppercase, between lowercase and between lowercase and uppercase, and study the type of curves, their anatomy, the presence of symmetry and the degrees of synthesis.

With a ruler and a compass it is possible to draw all the letters in this work. Each sheet is perfectly traced with the points of the compass.

CHAPTER 2

Letter Anatomy

Letter Anatomy

In order to clearly and precisely define a letter, different parts are distinguished in it, whose names are sometimes similar to those of human anatomy.

After consolidating the upper and lower case systems, the modifications in the shape of the letters have been of a practical order or following fashion, but the structure of each group of signs has been preserved over time. Although the structural differences between the two systems are wide and notorious, some relationships can be established:

Baseline

It is the imaginary horizontal line on which almost all the letters rest.

Not all of them follow the following criteria regarding the baseline:

• Capital letters sit just above the baseline. The most common exceptions appear in the letters J and Q where a tail exceeds the baseline.

• Punctuation marks and special characters are supported by the baseline with the exception of "¿¡,;", also the numbers 3 4 5 7 9 tend to descend the line.

• The lowercase are also found in it: g j p q and that you have antlers that also exceed the baseline and are called: descending antlers.

• Characters that have rounded strokes at the bottom (0 3 5 6 8 c C G J or O Q U) tend to extend slightly above the baseline to create the optical illusion that they are just above it, approximately 1.5%.

The vertical distance between two consecutive baselines in a paragraph is called the line height, although this term can also be applied to the distance between baselines minus the size of the font.

Capital Height

It is the height of the upper or upper case letters; it is measured from the baseline to the top of the uppercase character.

x-Height

x -height or body size refers to the distance between the baseline and the midline. Generally it was the height of the type corresponding to the lowercase letter x, (where the term comes from) and also of the u, v, w and z. Rounded letters such as a, c, e, m, n, o, r, and s tend to slightly exceed the height of the x. In modern typography it is a mere design parameter, although the x is usually that height, but in manual or decorative calligraphy styles this is not always the case.

Ascendants and descendants has an important role when it comes to recognizing the characters and fixing the image of the word, and thanks to them we can distinguish one form from another, such as h from n.

It therefore seems that a small x height increases the white space between lines and emphasizes the image of the text line, while an x height that is too large can hinder the reading speed as it unifies the image of the line. But there are studies that conclude that types with a large but moderate height of the x are generally more legible in small bodies than others. It seems that increasing the height of the x increases readability as if it were a larger body type. Thus it happens that different fonts can have a similar readability if they are presented with the same height of x.

Economic necessity historically leads to trying to insert more characters on a line and more lines on a page. From scribes with the use of Gothic writing, through the printer who must reduce costs and make portable books to web designers who try to insert the maximum content on the screen to avoid having to change it.

Ancient calligraphers was the pioneers in starting to modify the height of the x in order to save the text. Between 1557 and 1559 they cut the Philisophie Romaine type that had the height of the x slightly greater than the Garamond type common at the time. In this way, it was possible to compose texts in smaller bodies that were as legible as those of other typefaces composed in larger bodies.

Fonts with a large x height relative to the body have short ascendants and descendants. With a ruler equal to the size of the body, the text has a heavy appearance, it gives a too dark gray, it lacks white. On the other hand, fonts with a small x height, with long ascendants and descendants give a much lighter gray. To compensate for this effect, fonts with a large x height must increase the leading, which partially cancels out the space savings achieved by increasing the x height.

The use that will be made of a typeface or type will mark the proportions of its characters. For a text font, the ancestors must be large enough, even higher than the height of the capital letters, to allow you to easily distinguish one character from another.

Too small a height of the x may not be appropriate for a text typeface, but for a headline it may be a wise decision.

In the fine and black versions of the same type, the height of the x of the black must be higher than that of the fine, because if they are the same, the black version will appear optically smaller than the fine when they are combined in the same line of text.

Capital letters whose height is greater than the height of x because they have descending strokes that exceed the baseline are y, g, q, and p, they have lower tails, or they have ascendants that exceed the height of x such as l, k, byd, upper-tail letters. The relationship between the height of the x and the height of the body is one of the main characteristics that define the appearance of a typeface.

This distance determines the size (body) of the letter.

Ascender Line

It is the imaginary line reached by the upper ends of the ascending features of the lower case letters, which in some families coincide with the line of capital letters and in others they do not.

Descender Line

It is the imaginary line to which the lower ends of the descending features of the low box letters reach.

Ápice

Es la punta en la que termina la letra «A» mayúscula.

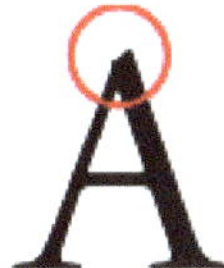

Apófige o cartela

Es la pequeña parte curva, generalmente de 1/4 de círculo, que enlaza el asta vertical con los terminales o remates.

Stem

A straight vertical stroke (or the main straight diagonal stroke in a

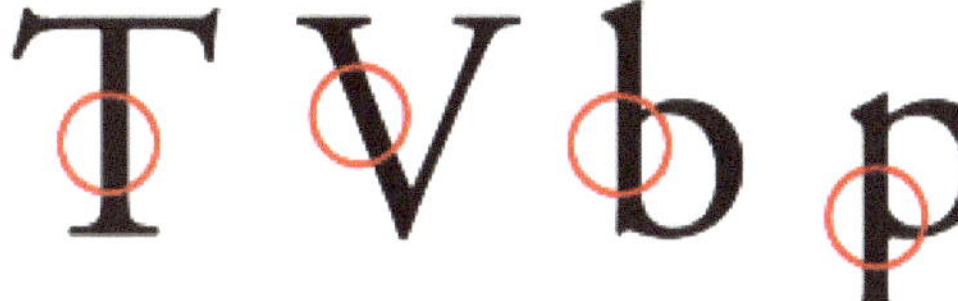

- Asta ascendente: asta de la letra que sobresale por encima de la altura x, como en la b, la d o la k.

- Asta descendente: asta de la letra que queda por debajo de la línea de base, como en la p o en la g.

- Spine: The main curved stroke of the S.

- Bar: The horizontal stroke in characters such as A, H, R, e, and f.

Arm

An upper or lower stroke that is attached on one end and free on the other.

Contraforma

Espacio total o parcialmente encerrado dentro de una letra.

Bowl

A curved stroke which creates an enclosed space within a character (the space is then called a counter).

Tail

The descender of a Q or short diagonal stroke of an R.

Sholder

The curved stroke of the h, m, n.

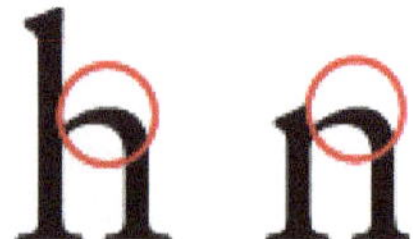

Croos

Horizontal line of the letters «T», «t» and «f»

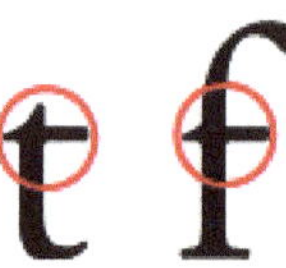

Neck

Line that joins the head with the tail of the «g».

Spur

A small projection off a main stroke found on many capital Gs

Arc

Finishing that is generally found
in the curved lines of the head of
some lowercase letters, for example
"a", "f" and "c".

Loop

The lower portion of the lowercase
g.

Vértice

Unión aguda y recta de dos trazos.

Ear

The small stroke that projects from
the top of the lowercase g.

Serif

Complementary element of the
Stem of the letters that carry it.

The Drawing of the Letters

Letter A

The letter A has two diagonal Stems, a thick one on the right and a thin one on the left, which are located at an apex that slightly exceeds the line of capital letters, this discrete optical correction is essential for the visual balance of the letter when it is it is preceded or succeeded by other characters, otherwise it would give the optical illusion that it is less than the other letters. The apex may end with a left finial, such as a concave cut or a horizontal cut. The horizontal bar is well below the center, so that this creates a balance between the interior counterforms

Letter B

The letter B shares characteristics of the E and the O, the stem is identical to that of the E, and the lobes basically follow the proportions of the O, The optical center is almost the same as the E. As in all the letters of two lobes, although geometrically equal, the lower one appears to be larger than the upper one. In order to correct this optical effect, the upper lobe must be smaller. Thus, the density of the upper lobe must also be less than that of the lower one, but the thickness must be greater than that of the Stem. The counterforms of the lobes are sometimes identical to D. B and E are practically the same width.

Letter C

To draw a C, we will take an O as a reference and cut it. The cutting point is essential, the midpoint of the right stroke is ideal, but it can be cut either to the right or to the left of this point.

As weight has been removed from the letter, it is necessary to compensate a little of that loss to try to balance the visual tension when compared to other letters. Weight should be added in the lower half adding more stability to the baseline and finials in the upper and lower part.

The top finial must be greater than the end of the E. Since the weight of the ring of the C is greater than that of the shaft of the E. a small spur with or without gusset can be added to add more density to the letter.

Letter D

The letter D is a combination of the E with the O, the shaft is identical to the E but the ring is not identical to the O since it does not exceed the baseline or the height of the capital letters.

The D in both the classical and modern systems is narrower than O

The counter form is sometimes attached to the flagpole with a finish giving it the shape of a tear. When the union is gross, the counterform is rational and contrasted.

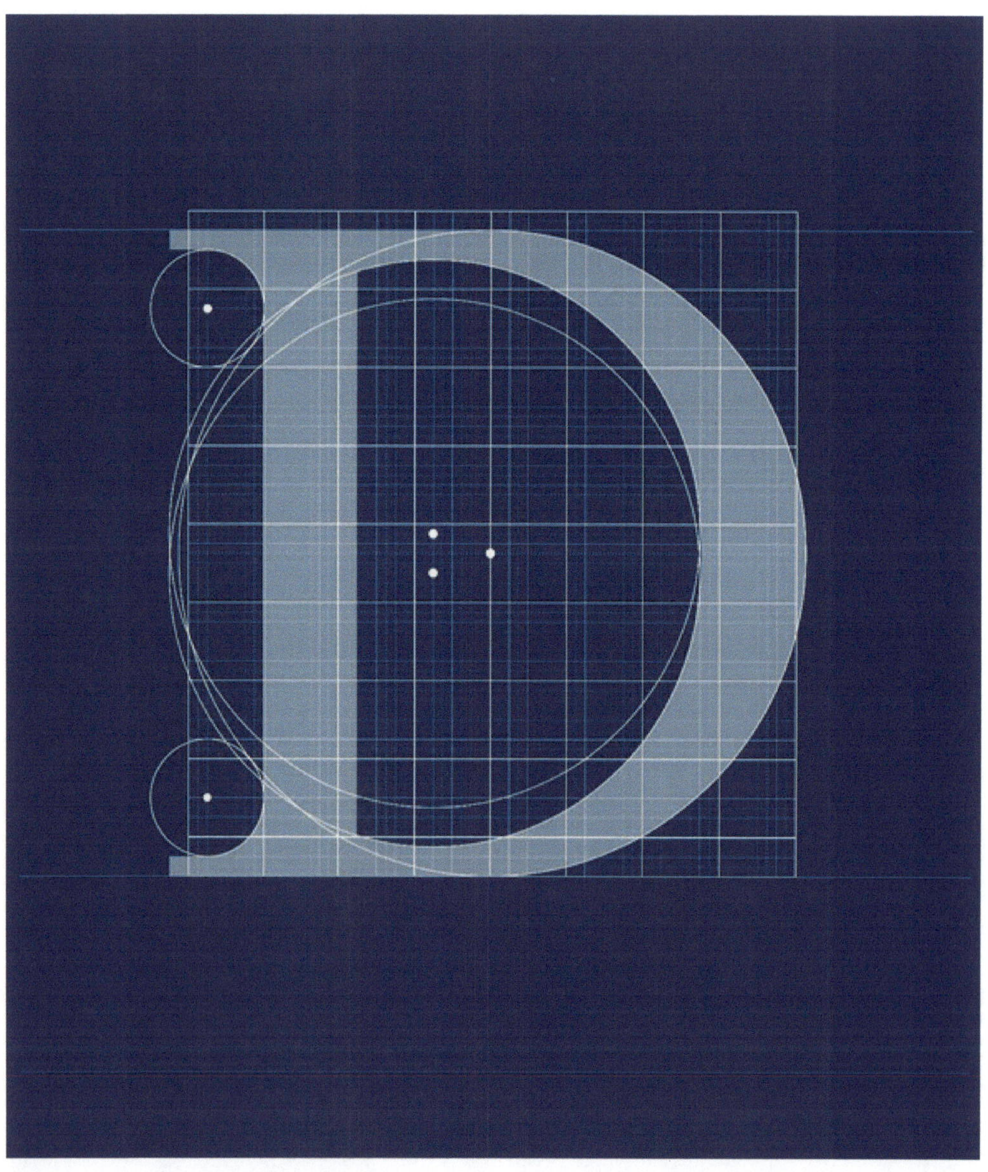

Letter E

In the E are many of the characteristics that define the font, such as: the proportional system, the visual center, the width of the vertical pole, style of the finishes and the serifs.

The vertical stem is not as wide as the maximum width of the O ring to provide visual balance.

The length of the arms varies: the central arm is shorter, the lower arm is longer, that serves to avoid the overlap of these, and to give balance in the density of the areas of the letter.

The optical center is slightly higher than the geometric center and the shaft has two finishers on the left called finish finishers

Letter F

The width without serrations is about ½ the height and is almost like an E without the lower arm. In some sources it is identical to E.

We clearly see in the evolution of the letter, a strong trend in the increase in the size of the balance finials, especially that of the upper arm and the loss of the central arm finial as we see in some Egyptian fonts.

Letter G

The letter G looks a lot like C, but its ring and serifs are not the same. Since there is a vertical neck on the G that adds weight. To reduce this visual density, you have to draw the top finish to the lower than in C and refine the ring in the upper right or lower left.

The neck should be drawn below the optical center to avoid excess visual load, but for optimum stability with the baseline, this neck can be drawn somewhat thicker than the main shaft.

The neck lines up with the top finial, but if the letter cut is made further to the left of the midpoint of the O ring, the resulting G has an exaggerated visual load compared to a C, therefore there is than to expand its internal counterform beyond the neck beyond the line of the upper auction.

Letter H

The width without serifs is about ¾ of the height. It is made up of two vertical stems attached to a horizontal bar above the geometric center, to balance the open counterforms.

Letter I

The I is a basic modular shape and is about 1/8 the height.

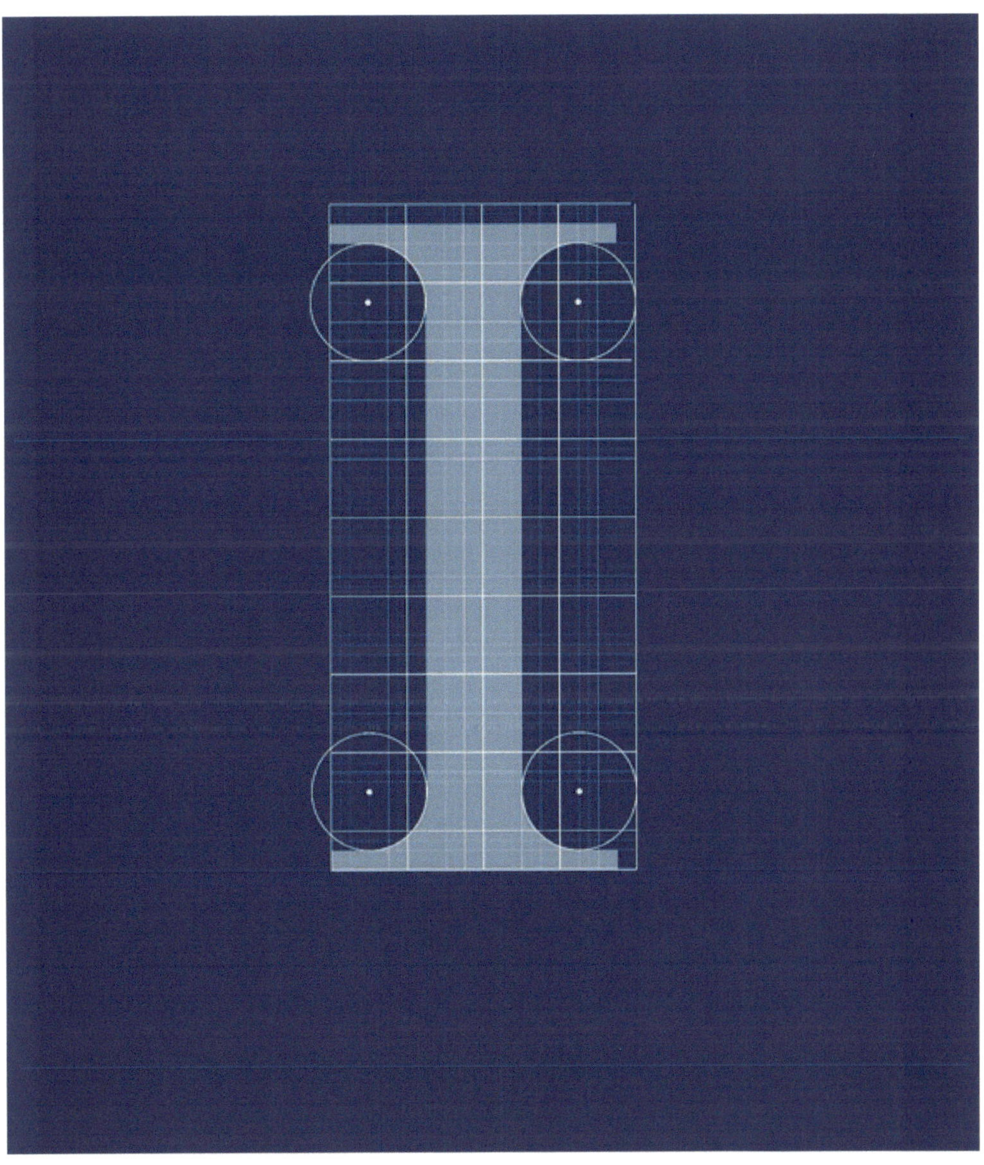

Letter J

The J is essentially a modified I with a left curved stroke at the bottom. There is no rule for its drawing, but its shape shows us which family the font belongs to. If the tail recalls calligraphic strokes then it refers to the classic family. If the tail has rounded or straight shapes, it reminds us of modern ones.

Originally, in the Latin alphabet the J was a calligraphic variant of the i, that is, an 'i' with an tail and was added in the Middle Ages.

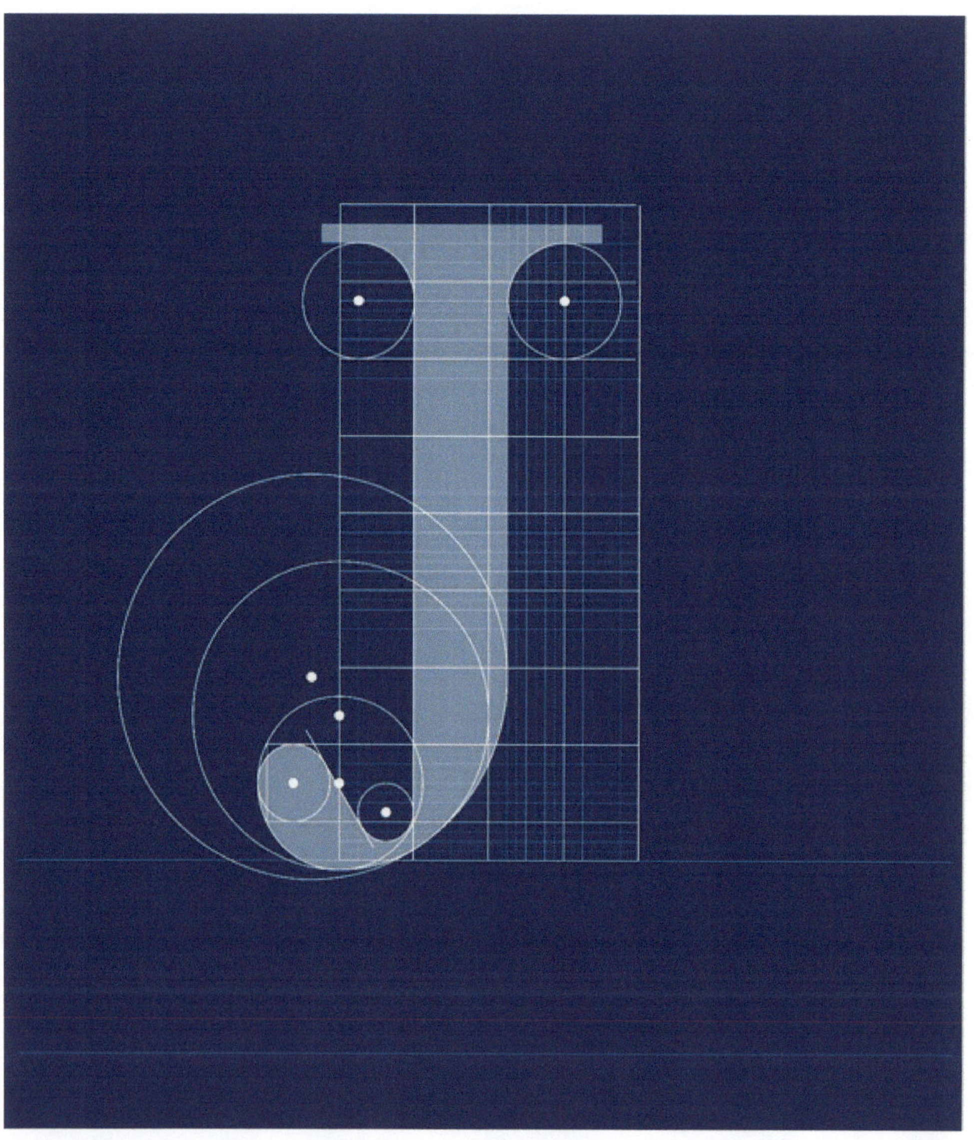

Letter K

The width without serifs is 5/8 of the height. the upper diagonal arm starts below the geometric center and should not go up to the 5/8 limit.

The lower arm begins above the center and extends to the limit of the width. That means that the upper part is less than the lower part like B and the angle of both arms is practically the same.

In human family the diagonals usually start exactly at the optic center.

Letter L

The width is ½ the height and almost identical to an E without the center and top arm. The bottom auction tends to grow in ancient families..

Letter M

The width is almost equal to the height. The vertices exceed the baseline, as the apex of the A exceeds the line of the capital letters, but there are cases in which they do not, as in heavy letters or in mechanical ones.

The stems in the classic families are not vertical, they have a slight inward inclination, in the modern ones there is almost no inclination whatsoever, they are generally vertical stems with outward finishing finishes at the top.

Letter N

The width without serifs is approximately ¾ of the height, in the classic and in the modern ones somewhat smaller, and in the mechanical ones the proportion is as in the classic ones.

The lower vertex must go over the base line, otherwise it would appear smaller when preceded or followed by other letters. But sometimes the diagonal rests on the baseline as in mechanical or very dark lettering.

The left stem ends with a large serif to the left.

Letter O

In the first types with serifs, more specifically in the classic Venetians and Garalds, the O was an almost perfect circle, with low contrast and angular modulation.

In the transients, the shape becomes oval, lowering in contrast and vertical, raising the modulation.

In modern ones, like the didonas, the contrast reaches its maximum, as well as the modulation that is now strictly vertical. In the mechanics the contrast varies, but follows the vertical modulation.

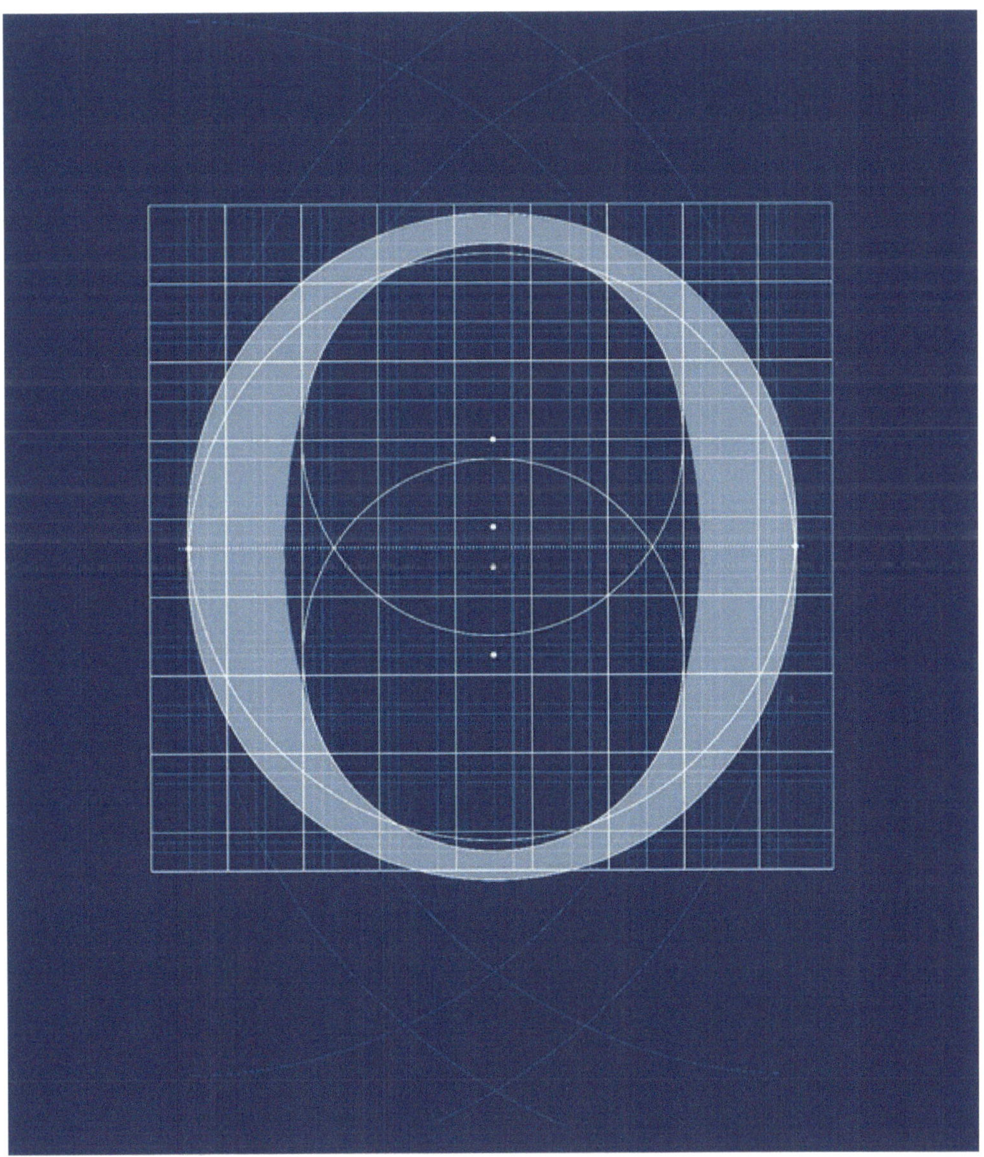

Letter P

These letters are closely related to B, but there are slight but expressive differences between the two.

The lobe of the P is larger, the inner part is usually horizontal, but in fonts with strong calligraphic influences it can be rounded when joining the stem or rather not joining it.

Letter Q

It is like an O with a tail whose tail varies its shape and size, in humans families it tends to be longer with a marked calligraphic influence and decreases in size until it reaches in mechanics with tails that are generally discrete in shape. and in its size.

Letter R

The size of the lobe of the R is between those of the b and the P. The tail can be a diagonal or a vertical arc. When the end of the tail is in the shape of an arch, it ends with a serif to the right or a spur that is the vestige of calligraphy

The left side of the tail never has a serif, and the inside finish of the shaft is usually smaller to avoid congestion at the baseline.

When the tail is diagonally it must go beyond the edge of the ring but care must be taken, an excessively large tail can cause spacing problems with letters in front of the R.

Letter S

It is a letter with two lobes, so follow the same rule: the bottom is bigger than the top. And the top and bottom circular shapes slightly exceed the baseline.

The serifs change, in the Venetian ones with a strong calligraphic influence, the finials remind us of the stroke of a pen, in the garalds we see the appearance of a spur, a characteristic that is repeated in most of the following families.

Letter T

The width is ¾ of the height, its top serifd have changed. In Venetian styles, the serifs generally have spurs and these serifs are sometimes sharp. In the garalds there is a tendency to lose the spurs and the loss of the angular shape. In the real ones, the serifs are mostly straight and the dewclaws tend to disappear.

In the modern ones there are no longer spurs, the finials are perfectly straight.

Letter U

The width is 4/4 of the height, and there are two U-shapes, one with two thick stems and a straight monoremate on the right stem. And one with a thick stem on the left and a thin one on the right.

The curve exceeds the baseline while when there is the serif, it follows the baseline,

In some families of letters there is a tendency to stand out in the form without a lower serif. In modern ones, the monorematted form does not appear while it is very common in Venetian ones.

Letter V

The width is ¾ of the height, and it hardly changes. The vertex exceeds the baseline in almost all families with the exception of mechanics where it follows the baseline, or in very dense styles in other families.

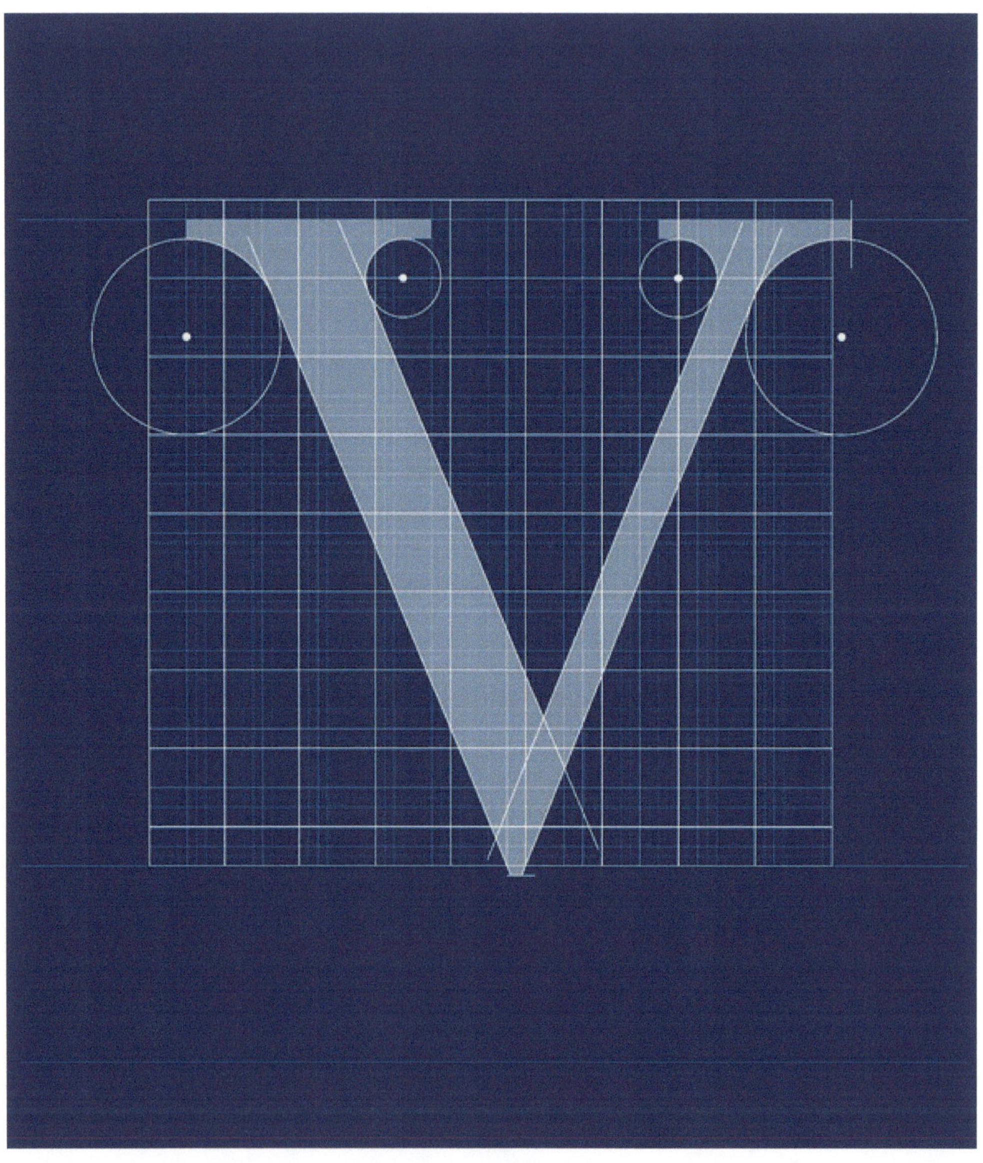

Letter W

The width and height are the same. It is formed by ligature, that is, it is the fusion of two intersecting letters V. The crossing point varies, but the tendency is for the shapes to meet in a central point with a joining finish.

The vertices exceed the baseline, except in the mechanics where there is a cut in the baseline as in very dark styles from other families.

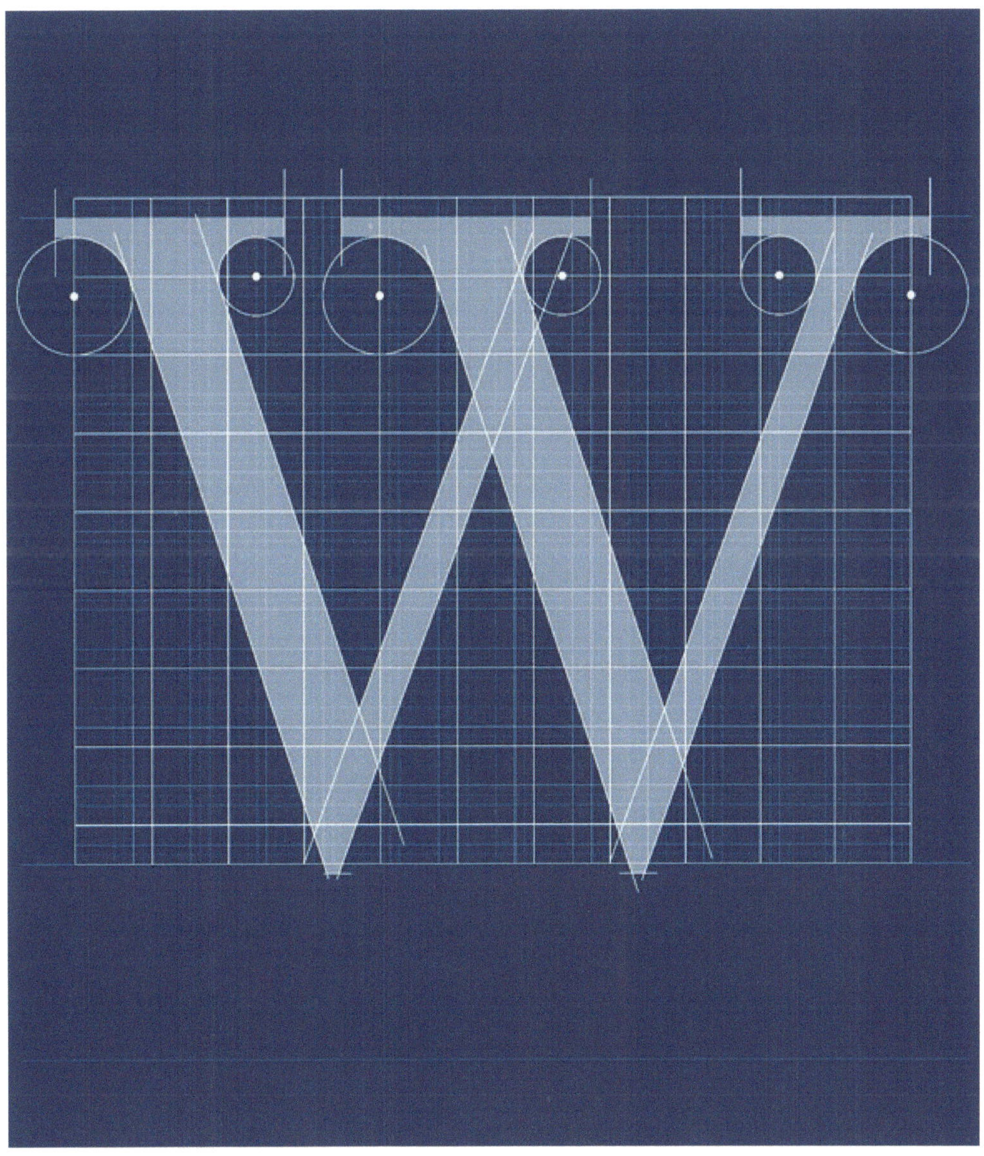

Letter X

The width is ¾ of the height. The crossing point of the stem is somewhat above the geometric center, making the upper part smaller than the lower one, providing visual balance.

Letter Y

The width is ¾ of the height. The junction point of the three strokes is slightly below the optical center. The point can be lower to improve balance with neighboring letters.

There were no significant changes..

Letter Z

The width is ¾ of the height. Z is not a Roman letter so the diagonal stroke is different in the opposite direction from the other thick strokes of the other letters.

The horizontal strokes end with vertical serifs.

Glossary

A

all caps
Text or a font in which all letters are capital letters.

B

boldface
A font that is dark, having a high ration of ink to white space, written or drawn with thick strong lines.

F

face
A typeface.

font
A set of glyphs of unified design, belonging to one typeface (such as Helvetica), style (such as italic), and weight (such as bold). Examples: Georgia Regular, Futura Book Oblique, Univers 47.

font family
(used in computer typography) A typeface; face.

G

glyph
A visual representation of a letter, character, or symbol, in a specific font and style.

I

italics
Letters in an italic typeface.

J

justification
The alignment of text to the left margin (left justification), the right margin (right justification), or both margins (full justification).

K

kern
The overhang of one letter to another letter which affects the spacing of characters. Kerning is altered to make text more clear.

L

ligature
The conflation of two characters to avoid collisions or facilitate legibility.

R

running text
The body of text, as distinct from headings, footnotes, diagrams and other added material.

S

A serif font and a sans serif one
sans serif
A typeface in which the characters do not have serifs.
sentence case
The standard capitalisation of an English sentence, with the first letter uppercase and subsequent letter lowercase with exceptions such as proper nouns or acronyms.
serif
A short horizontal line added to the tops and bottoms of traditional typefaces, such as Times Roman.

A small caps font
small caps
Capital letters A, B, C, ... shown in the same form but in small size (typically of the same size as lower-case letters).
T
title case
The capitalization in which the first letter of each major word is set in capital, used for titles and headings.
typeface
A set of fonts of a unified design, typically combining several weights (such as light, medium, bold), styles (roman, italic), or widths (narrow, extended). A face; font family. Examples: Frutiger, Garamond, Helvetica.
typesetting
The setting or composition of written material into type.
typography
The art or practice of setting and arranging type; typesetting.
W
weight
The boldness of a font; the relative thickness of its strokes, such as light, medium, book, bold, or heavy.